GEMINI

Published in 2024
by Gemini Children's Books Ltd
Part of Gemini Books Group

Based in Woodbridge and London

Marine House, Tide Mill Way
Woodbridge, Suffolk, IP12 1AP
United Kingdom

www.geminibooks.com

Copyright © 2024 Gemini Children's Books Ltd

EU Authorised Representative, Vulcan Consulting,
38/39 Fitzwilliam Square West, Dublin 2, D02 NX53, Ireland

All rights reserved. No part of this publication may be
reproduced, stored in a retrieval system, or transmitted in any
form or by any means, electronically, mechanical, photocopying,
recording, or otherwise, without the prior permission of the
copyright owners and the publishers.

A CIP catalogue record for this book is available from the British Library.

ISBN 978 1 91708 208 2

Printed in Guangdong, China
10 9 8 7 6 5 4 3 2 1

Bear's Book of Calm

Written by
Seb Davey

Illustrated by
Julia Seal

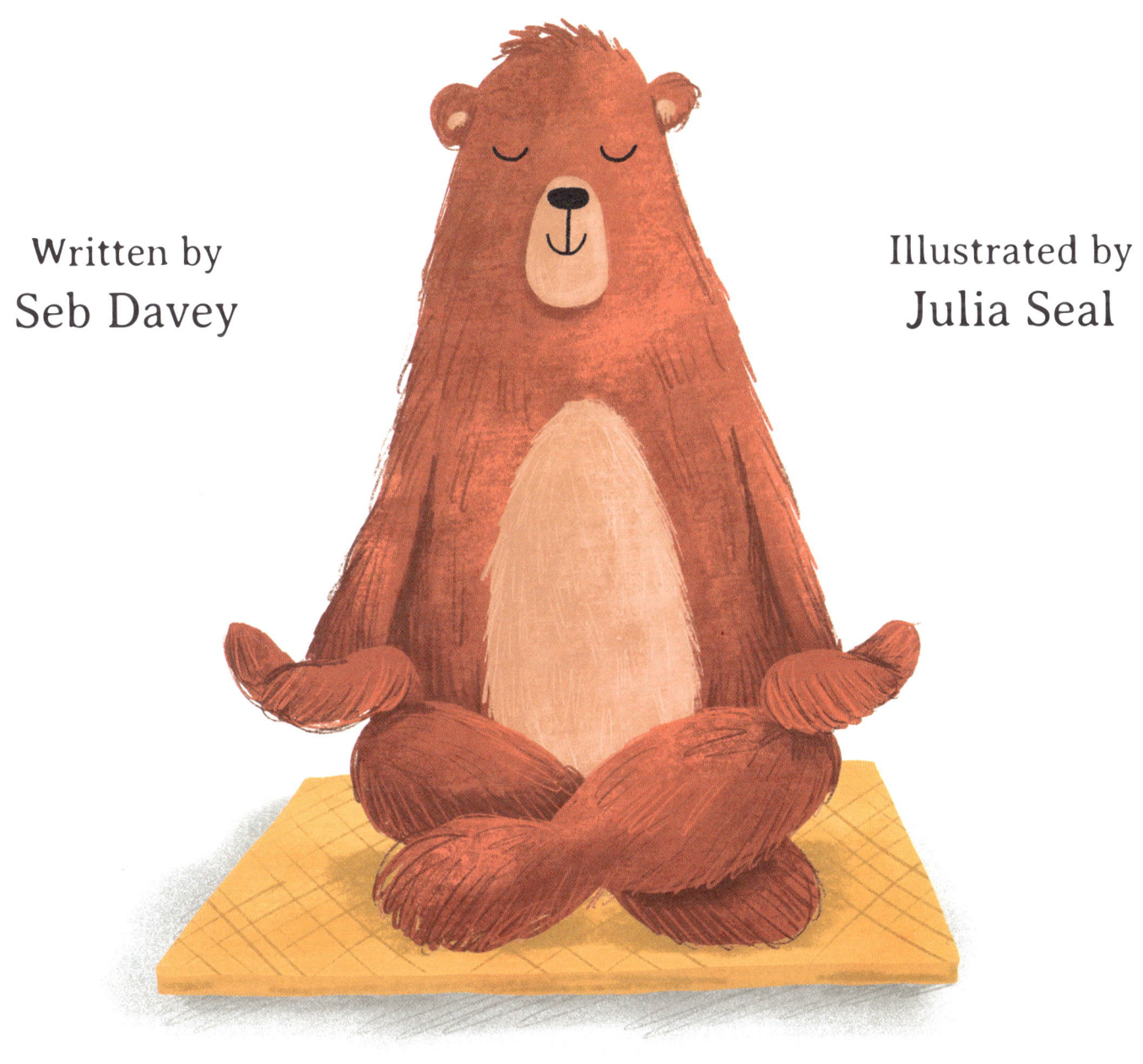

Breathe. Count 1.

Calm.

Be still ...

It's good to take things slow sometimes.

Breathe. Count 2.

Listen.

Really listen ...

What can you hear?

Breathe. Count 3.

Look.

Notice things ...

What can you see?

Step outside ...

Feel the air on your skin.

Breathe. Count 5. **Hug.**

You're not alone …

Enjoy the warmth of being together.

Breathe. Count 6.

Eat.

Take your time ...

Taste and appreciate every flavour.

Breathe. Count 7.

Talk.

Be open and honest …

Share feelings with yourself and others.

Breathe. Count 8.

Share.

Share with your heart ...

Show your family that you care about them.

Breathe. Count 9.

Focus.

Dream big ...

You can follow your dreams.

Breathe. Count 10.

Exercise.

Clear your thoughts ...
        Enjoy and notice your surroundings.

Breathe.
Count 11.

Be quiet.

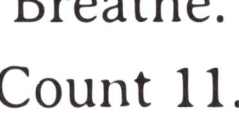

Listen to the sound
of your heart ...

Let everything else
drift away.

Breathe. Count 12.

Smile.

Be happy in the moment ...

Remember the good things about your day.

Calm. Listen. Look. Feel.

Hug. Eat. Talk. Share.

Focus. Exercise. Be quiet. Smile.